First Facts®

PREDATOR PROFILES

EAGLES
— BUILT FOR THE HUNT —

by Tammy Gagne

Consultant: Dr. Jackie Gai, DVM
Wildlife Veterinarian

CAPSTONE PRESS
a capstone imprint

First Facts are published by Capstone Press,
1710 Roe Crest Drive, North Mankato, Minnesota 56003
www.mycapstone.com

Library of Congress Cataloging-in-Publication Data
Gagne, Tammy, author.
Eagles : built for the hunt / by Tammy Gagne.
pages cm.—(First facts. Predator profiles)
Audience: Ages 6-9.
Audience: K to grade 3.
Summary: "Describes the features, behaviors, and adaptations that make eagles skilled
predators"—Provided by publisher.
Includes bibliographical references and index.
ISBN 978-1-4914-8842-3 (library binding)
ISBN 978-1-4914-8844-7 (eBook PDF)
1. Eagles—Juvenile literature. 2. Predation (Biology)—Juvenile literature. I. Title.
QL696.F32G34 2016
598.9′42—dc23   2015020219

Editorial Credits
Carrie Braulick Sheely, editor; Sarah Bennett and Juliette Peters, designers;
Tracy Cummins, media researcher; Tori Abraham, production specialist

Photo Credits
Getty Images: George Silk/Time & Life Pictures, 19, Guy Edwardes, 15; Shutterstock:
Bildagentur Zoonar GmbH, 14, Capture Light, Cover, davemhuntphotography, 3, Donjiy,
12, FloridaStock, 5, Jean-Edouard Rozey, 21, martellostudio, 13, Nachiketa Bajaj, 6, Neil
Burton, 8-9, ODM Studio, 16, Peter Krejzl, Cover Back, Peter Wey, 2, piotrwzk, 17, Sergey
Uryadnikov, 10-11, Serjio74, 1, worldswildlifewonders, 7

Printed and bound in China.

007479LEOS16
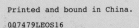

TABLE OF CONTENTS

WASTING NO TIME

The lake water is barely moving. But the sharp-eyed eagle spots the salmon just below the water's surface. The hungry bird swoops down. Dipping only its feet into the water, the eagle grabs the fish with its long **talons**.

Eagles are among the world's most powerful **predators**. They are called birds of **prey** or raptors because they mainly hunt other animals for food.

talon—a long, sharp claw
predator—an animal that hunts other animals for food
prey—an animal hunted by another animal for food
species—a group of animals with similar features

DON'T BE PICKY!

Eagles live where they can get food. Most eagles nest on cliffs or in the tops of tall trees. They can see prey better from up above. Many eagles live close to water where fish such as salmon, herring, and catfish are plentiful. Eagles also eat smaller birds and land animals such as rabbits. The harpy eagle is the largest eagle species. It eats monkeys and sloths. Some eagles will even feast on **carrion** left behind by other predators.

FACT

The serpent eagle is named for the prey it hunts. This species eats **reptiles** such as snakes, frogs, and lizards.

serpent eagle

carrion—dead, rotting flesh

reptile—a cold-blooded animal that breathes air and has a backbone; most reptiles have scales

harpy eagle

CLEVER HUNTERS

Eagles hunt during the day. Most eagles hunt alone. But sometimes two bald eagles will pair up to make the job easier. One bird flies near the ground to **flush** small birds from trees and bushes. The other eagle perches nearby so it can snatch the prey from the air. Once the prey has been caught, the eagles share the meal.

FACT

Some eagles even walk along the ground and grab prey out of holes.

flush—to cause to take flight suddenly

STEALING FOOD

Eagles sometimes steal fish from other birds. An eagle will chase and pester the other bird in midair. It won't let up until the other predator drops its kill. Often the eagle will then catch the prey in its talons while it is still falling.

FACT

Bald eagles have been known to steal fish off people's fishing rods.

AN EYE FOR THE HUNT

Eagles have excellent eyesight. They can see both in front of them and to each side at the same time. Just as important, eagles can see objects both near and far away. A golden eagle can spot a rabbit from up to 1 mile (1.6 km) away.

FACT
An eagle's vision is at least four times sharper than a person's.

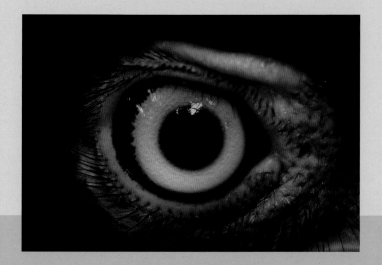

FAST IN FLIGHT

Eagles are fast fliers. Golden eagles are the fastest eagles. While flying level through the air, they can reach 80 miles (129 km) per hour. Once a golden eagle spots prey, it's time for the big dive! A golden eagle can dive at speeds of up to 200 miles (322 km) per hour.

FACT
Bald eagles can dive at speeds near 100 miles (161 km) per hour.

a golden eagle in flight

A golden eagle grabs for its prey.

MEAL TIME

Eagles kill prey with their sharp talons. These powerful claws rip through animal flesh like knives. Eagles also rely on their hooked beaks for tearing flesh off their kills. Since they have no teeth, eagles swallow these chunks of meat whole.

FACT

A **myth** says that once an eagle grabs prey with its talons, the eagle can't let go. This idea that the talons lock around the prey isn't true. But few prey animals can escape an eagle's powerful grip.

myth—a false idea that many people believe

STRONG IN BODY AND MIND

The largest eagles can carry more than 10 pounds (4.5 kilograms). Some eagles put their strength to the test. A fish that weighs more than 5 pounds (2.3 kg) is too heavy for a bald eagle to carry. Yet this eagle doesn't just give up. Many bald eagles will swim to shore with the prey instead of flying with it. They use their wings as paddles.

FACT

Some bald eagles are too stubborn for their own good. They drown trying to lift fish that are too heavy.

GROWING UP

Baby eagles are called eaglets. After **fledging,** the young birds learn to fly. While they practice flying, the parents bring back food to the nest. Eaglets learn to hunt by watching the adults. The young birds will grow up to be some of the most powerful predators in the world.

FACT
Eagles often use the same nest each year.

AMAZING BUT TRUE!

Bald eagles are known for building huge nests. It might take a pair of bald eagles at least two weeks to build their nest. The largest bald eagle nest ever found measured 9.5 feet (3 meters) wide and 20 feet (6 m) high. This incredible dwelling weighed more than 2 tons (1.8 metric tons)! That's equal to the weight of about four adult polar bears!

fledge—to develop the feathers needed for flying

GLOSSARY

carrion (KAR-ee-uhn)—dead, rotting flesh

fledge (FLEJ)—to develop the feathers needed for flying

flush (FLUHSH)—to cause to take flight suddenly

level (LEV-uhl)—at the same height

myth (MITH)—a false idea that many people believe

predator (PRED-uh-ter)—an animal that hunts other animals for food

prey (PRAY)—an animal hunted by another animal for food

reptile (REP-tile)—a cold-blooded animal that breathes air and has a backbone; most reptiles have scales

species (SPEE-sheez)—a group of animals with similar features

talon (TAL-uhn)—a long, sharp claw, especially the claw of a bird of prey

READ MORE

George, Jean Craighead. *The Eagles Are Back.* New York: Dial Books for Young Readers, 2013.

Llanas, Sheila Griffin. *Bald Eagles.* Animal Icons. Minneapolis: ABDO Pub., 2013.

Riggs, Kate. *Eagles.* Seedlings. Mankato, Minn.: Creative Education, 2015.

INTERNET SITES

FactHound offers a safe, fun way to find Internet sites related to this book. All of the sites on FactHound have been researched by our staff.

Here's all you do:

Visit *www.facthound.com*

Type in this code: 9781491488423

Super-cool stuff!

Check out projects, games and lots more at
www.capstonekids.com

CRITICAL THINKING USING THE COMMON CORE

1. Explain how the areas where eagles live help them find food. (Key Ideas and Details)

2. Name three features that help eagles catch their prey. Which one of these do you think is most important? Why? (Integration of Knowledge and Ideas)

INDEX